WOMEN
MATTER
TO GO

Published in the United states of America
ISBN: 9798787873177
Imprint: Independently published

Nonfiction > Religion > Christian Education > Adult
Nonfiction > Religion > Sexuality & Gender Studies

Cover: original oil painting by Ann Boland

TABLE OF CONTENTS

INTRODUCTION

Who can find a virtuous woman?
for her price is far above rubies.

Proverbs 31:10

In the creation account from the book of Genesis it is an indisputable fact that God created both men and women in His image.[1]
Neither of them received more or less than the other. So the Bible begins on the basis of equality. Each were made as an individual person, spiritual being, and human being. Both were made equal thus both should be just as caring, reassuring, compassionate, understanding, encouraging, and cooperative with each other and others.[ii]

Due to many factors, women have customarily fulfilled a supportive role to the male in her life, her family, and church. She seems to have gained joy and a sense of accomplishment from being a wife, mother, and church leader. The secular world has tried, and with some success, to influence many women into abandoning these roles by taking on a more assertive, masculine approach to life. Unfortunately, this has created chaos and confusion regarding the role of women in general. It is in itself a trademark of satanic forces. Only Scripture can expose God's real intent for the role and purpose of women.[iii]

Even though Jesus' named disciples were men, it is obvious that He surrounded himself with strong women.[iv] He even taught them.[v] He revealed that He was the Messiah to the Samaritan woman.[vi] He taught Lazarus sister Mary and admonished Martha by pointing out the priority of learning spiritual truth over what the world considered "womanly" responsibilities like serving guests in one's home.[vii]

It is true that Christian marriage emphasizes mutual love and submission between two believers.[viii] This is based on four passages in the New Testament which expressly gives wives the responsibility of submitting to their husbands.[ix] This idea of submission however is actually cooperative, co-equal, and mutually supportive. It is an expression of love for God and a desire to follow His design.[x] It should never be pictured as demeaning or in any way diminishing the female's place in the marriage and place of equality. It is tied to the **calling** of the male to love his wife "sacrificially" as Christ loved the church.[xi] It should make the male realize that he is **called** to serve the female as leader in a relationship of two equals. It should make him realize that he has been **called** to set the example of leadership before their children as to how to have a loving relationship with their mother and God.[xii] The females are urged to raise their own children at home which means that they are the managers of the household.[xiii]

From the very beginning, women fulfilled a vital role in the Christian church.[xiv] The disciples were all men. The chief missionary activity was done mainly by men. However, Scripture makes it clear that it is obvious that the underlining success of the very mission work they performed would not have been completely successful without the role of women. The writing of the New Testament was the work of men. The leadership in the churches was entrusted to men. However, let's not forget that the scripture is laden with the many roles that women played supporting, encouraging, and yes, even teaching others about the truth of Christ.

The Apostle Paul respected women and worked side by side with them for the furtherance of the gospel.[xv] However, we see nowhere in scripture that he ever appointed any female elders or pastors. In his letters, he urged that men were to be the leaders in the church. He established that women were not to teach or exercise authority over men.[xvi] That however did not limited their teaching ability to other women.

However, to be fair we must understand that God has used both genders for His purposes. He used the females in many different ways.[xvii]

- Miriam <u>help her brothers lead</u> Israel.[xviii]

- Shiphrah, Puah, Pharaoh's daughter and even Mephibosheth's <u>nurse disobeyed the legal authorities</u> of the day and jeopardize their own safety by rescuing young children from danger.[xix]

- In a similar incident Jehosheba <u>rescued</u> her nephew Joash.[xx]

- Women <u>served at the entrance to the tent of meeting and perform sacred duties</u> for the Israelites in a sacred space.[xxi]

- Zipporah, Abigail, and Michal were used by God to <u>save their husbands</u> from imminent death.[xxii]

- Tamar, an ancestor of Jesus Christ, dressed like a prostitute and bore a child through her father-in-law so that she could have legitimate children. She is even <u>praised</u> for this![xxiii]

- Rahab, another of Jesus Christ ancestors, <u>committed treason</u> against her own people in order to help Israel, and cut a shrewd deal to rescue her family.[xxiv]

- Mahlah, Tirzah, Hoglah, Milka and Noah (Zelophehad's daughters) <u>petitioned for their legal rights</u> of inheritance, and have their story told on three separate occasions in the Old Testament.[xxv]

- Deborah was only one of five women described as a <u>prophet</u> in the Old Testament. The four others are Miriam, Huldah, Noadiah, and "the prophetess."[xxvi]

- Jael the wife of Heber took a tent peg through the skull of Sisera <u>killing</u> him.[xxvii]

- Samson's mother, Nabal's wife Abigail, the woman of Shunem, and Zacharias' wife Elizabeth were all <u>more spiritually perceptive than their husbands</u>.[xxviii]

- Abigail and Jael <u>went against their husbands wishes</u> and are praised in the Bible for their heroic actions.

- The women <u>known as the wise women</u> of Abel Beth Maacah became the spokesperson and successfully negotiate with King David's general Joab for the deliverance of her town.

- Ruth, <u>based on the advice of her mother-in-law</u>, made the first move in securing a husband for herself by going to him at night and uncovering his "feet."[xxix]

- Huldah was not only a <u>prophetess</u> but a royal adviser too.[xxx]

- Sheerah is remembered for building a town and the daughters of Shallum are remembered for helping to <u>restore the walls</u> of Jerusalem.[xxxi]

- Women of royalty were The Queen of Sheba Candace and Esther.[xxxii]

- The widow of Zarephath <u>gave away</u> her son's last meagre meal to a prophet.

She did it even in the face of a severe famine, because that's what God had personally directed her to do.[xxxiii]

- There is the story of the young Jewish slave girl taken captive yet she <u>shared her faith</u> with the wife of her abductor which resulted in his being healed of leprosy.[xxxiv]

- Achsah was one of many women <u>successful involved in business, agriculture, and/or industry</u>.[xxxv]

- Miriam, Jephthah's daughter, and the wailing women in Jeremiah were a few of the many women who <u>led public, formal displays of celebration or mourning</u>.[xxxvi]

- Miriam, Deborah, Hannah, Mary, and Elizabeth all said <u>prophetic prayers and praises</u> that had the authority of holy scripture.[xxxvii]

- King Lemuel's Mother Priscilla, Anna, Lois and Eunice <u>taught theology and shared inspired messages</u>.[xxxviii]

- Women were the <u>first eyewitness</u> of Jesus' death, burial, and resurrection and told others about it.[xxxix]
- Lydia, Nympha, Priscilla, Aquila, and other women <u>hosted and led</u> house churches in the first century.[xl]

BLESSED

Her children arise up, and call her blessed;
her husband also, and he praise her.

Proverbs 31:28

Blessings are not handed out easily in the bible. So, what does it really mean to be blessed?[xli] According to the American Heritage College Dictionary the secular world believes it all comes down to happiness, pleasure, or contentment. On the other hand, thinking biblically, it meant to make holy, to sanctify, to show favor upon, or to honor.[xlii] The Greek word *makários,* which translates as "blessed" describes a someone as being in an enviable position for receiving God's favor. It further means having received God's grace.[xliii] Consider the following:

- In the beginning God *blessed* both the male and female. He instructed them on several occasions to be fruitful and multiply.[xliv]

- Rebekah's family *blessed* her before she left to marry Isaac.[xlv]

- Leah tried to "selfishly" proclaim herself blessed because she bore children and her sister Rachel did not.[xlvi]

- It was an ancient custom for the father to kiss and *bless* their sons and daughters.[xlvii]

- God promised to *bless*, protect, and love His people, both male and female. [xlviii]

- God promised a *blessing* over His people (both male and female). This carried over to their city, property, offspring, community, work, and businesses. It was only if and when they had a Godly relationship with Him.[xlix]

- The religious leaders *blessed* Jael, the wife of Heber the Kenite, for saving Israel from annihilation.[l]

- Boaz *blessed* Ruth because of her kindness.[li]

- The Jewish women *blessed* Naomi because the Lord did not abandon her.[lii]

- Eli *blessed* Elkanah and his wife because of their sacrifice of the child Samuel.[liii]

- David *blessed* Abigail for her actions in providing his troops with food and keeping him from destroying her family.[liv]
- A wife and mother is *blessed* and praised in Proverbs 31.[lv]
- King Solomon *blessed* and praised his wife in a song.[lvi]
- Mary, the mother of Jesus Christ, was identified as being *favored* and *blessed* among women by God's angel.[lvii]

BIBLE STUDY

Judges 5:24

Blessed above women shall Jael the wife of Heber the Kenite be, blessed shall she be above women in the tent.

Ruth 4:14

And the women said unto Naomi, Blessed be the Lord, which hath not left thee this day without a kinsman, that his name may be famous in Israel.

Luke 1:28

And the angel came in unto her, and said, Hail, thou that art highly favored, the Lord is with thee: blessed art thou among women.

Please answer the following questions:

- Why were these women considered blessed?
- What is the takeaway from these blessings for us?

WOMEN

BOLAND

APPEARANCE

"Don't touch this!"
"Don't eat that!"
"Don't handle the other!"
Such prohibitions are concerned with things meant to perish by being used [not by being avoided!]...they are based on man-made rules and teachings.
They do indeed have the outward appearance of wisdom, with their self-imposed religious observances, false humility and asceticism; but they have no value at all in restraining people from indulging their old nature.

Colossians 2:21-23 (CJB)

When I think of appearances I am drawn back to my youth ministry days. There once was a young lady who came to our Wednesday night activities on a regular basis. Let's say, for the most part she was inappropriately dressed. The pastor and deacon's called me into the office one night and made it a point that I should directly address this person and her clothing problem. I agreed but not in the manner that they wanted. In full disclosure, not only was I the youth minister I was also the high school history teacher. I saw and interacted with these young people every day, including this young person. I wore a suit and tie every day of the week at school, Wednesday night, and on Sunday. They saw me in this attire all the time. So, come the following Wednesday I changed my clothing to what one would call a homeless person. I was in rough shape. Torn dirty shirt, holey blue jeans. No socks. "Air-conditioned shoes" (seriously holey) and ruffed up hair. I was a mess. I walked into the youth room as if nothing were wrong. They noticed! They asked why I was dressed that way! They would not let it go. I ignored their questions. I acted as if nothing was wrong. I responded as if this was my normal attire. However, they continued to question me. The subject of the night was "doing our best for the Lord." Technically, it had nothing to do with clothing or appearance. It had more to do with attitude and conduct. I never responded to their inquiries or personal comments about my appearance. At the end of the night the last one to leave the room was that young lady. She stared at me all night long. Finally, she asked, "was this all for me and how I am dressed?" I looked at her and asked, "did I ever mention you, how you dressed or your name? Did the subject inappropriate ever come up?" She agreed I had said none of this. However, from that time on she changed the clothes she wore. She never wore anything inappropriate again. The youth group continually volunteered to burn those clothes I wore until I convinced them they were long gone.

The truth is, God wants us all to dress modestly all the time. The bible supports the idea of modest and appropriate dress for Christian attire for both males and females. Everything about us must display righteousness and faithfulness because we, as His witnesses, should reflect honor and glory upon God.

The scriptures clearly state that a woman must not dress masculine, nor a man dress feminine. The scripture makes it clear that the Lord "detests" anyone who does this and that is not how God designed us.[lviii] God refers to this as inappropriate attire. It is not about a church "dress code" it is simply what reflects Godly appropriateness. It is conduct that establishes decency and respectability within Christian community and separates us from the secular world.

Paul and Peter, in their treatise about what women should wear, cautioned them to separate themselves from the pagan world of their day. This is still good advice in our secular world. Women and men should dress modestly, based on self-worth, and innocence. Outward adornment should be not to impress the secular world but to keep one's self-respect.[lix] One's hairstyle should not be outlandish, ornate, or elaborate in order to impress others but seek to be natural as God intended whether one's hair is straight, curly, or something else. God always requires us to dress modestly and appropriately. The word modest (*Kosmos*) means orderly, well arranged and decent,[lx] or of good behavior.[lxi] The Messianic Jews state that a women "should be dressed modestly and sensibly in respectable attire, not with elaborate hairstyles and gold jewelry, or pearls, or expensive clothes. 10 Rather, they should adorn themselves with what is appropriate for women who claim to be worshipping God, namely, good deeds."[lxii]

In other words, it is not God's intention for us to wear expensive clothing but just look our best and beautiful. We should not cross the line of immoral or indecent fashion, make-up, or bling.[lxiii] We must display humility and the fear of God in every aspect of our lives. We should never expose or wear clothing that emphasizes private body parts, only that which honors God. [lxiv]

True believers in Christ know that physical attractiveness or beauty is not important. However, uncombed hair, and ripped unkept clothes, or a person who slouches are pretty good indication of how a person feels about him / herself. A person's outward appearance provides insight into that person's personality, if not their character.

For some, "looks" are everything. For others it refers only to their physical features. The vast majority of people judge others by their physical characteristics such as: clothes, personality style, hygiene, or posture. Many find attractiveness in areas that go beyond the physical, such as: sense of humor, shared interests, kindness, values, principals, safety, happiness, or attractiveness. Statistically, physical features have a lot to do with success.[lxv] Several surveys discovered how the secular world view appearance:

- Tall people got paid more money. The research found that for every inch of height, a tall worker can expect to earn more money per year.

- Fat people got paid less money. Obese workers (those who have a Body Mass Index of more than 30) are paid even less.[lxvi]

- Obese women are more likely to be discriminated against when it comes to pay, hiring and raises.

- Blondes got paid more![lxvii] There has to be a joke in there somewhere.

- Workers who exercise get paid more.[lxviii] workers who exercise regularly earn nine percent more on average than employees who don't work out. Those who exercise three or more get paid more than their slothful coworkers.[lxix]

- Women who wear makeup make more: Not only do people judge beauty based on how much makeup a woman is wearing, but make-up adorned women also rank higher in competence and trustworthiness.[lxx]

- Handsome people are paid more, while unattractive employees miss out.[lxxi]

- Attractive people do better at salary and hiring. Attractive men always enjoy an advantage. Attractive women faced discrimination when applying for "masculine" jobs.[lxxii]

- People judged physical strength based on facial bone structure.

- Women and young workers were more likely to face appearance discrimination.

- Young girls in a single-sex environment tend to be more confident, more willing to share opinions, and more likely to develop a passion for Stem subjects (science, technology, engineering and mathematics).

It is unfortunate but we live in such a world where people judge others by their looks. Appearance needs to be kept in perspective.

The Bible tells us that it is important to present ourselves as nicely as possible, but God does not call us to go to extremes.[lxxiii] It is important that we remain aware of why we do the things we do not to look good before others but to bring honor and glory to God.[lxxiv]

BIBLE STUDY

1 Samuel 16:7

But the Lord said unto Samuel,

1. Look not on countenance,
2. Look not on the height of stature,
3. For man looks on the outward appearance;
4. For the Lord sees not as man sees,
5. The Lord looks on the heart.

Matthew 23:28

1. Even so you also outwardly appear righteous unto men;
2. Within you are full of hypocrisy and iniquity.

Please answer the following question:
- Why is appearance important?

WOMEN

BOLAND

EQUALITY

There is neither Jew nor Greek,
There is neither bond nor free,
There is neither male nor female,
For you are all one in Christ Jesus.

Galatians 3:28

What is equality, really? What does it mean to be equal? In a 2013 secular Pew survey respondents were divided on the question of how equal men and women were in today's society. Forty percent say society treats men and women equally; but forty-five percent said society favors men over women.[lxxv] The Bible's message is quite clear about the equality of men and women in marriage and church. The bible consistently affirms the equal status of men and women.[lxxvi] Unfortunately, secular society does not!

Equality is defined as a state of being. Equality is having the same quantity, amount, measure, or value one to another.[lxxvii] Equality is one of our central democratic principles. Equality is based on the belief that all people have the same opportunities to be successful, productive, and enjoy life. Equality is where each individual or group is given the same resources necessary to overcome whatever life throws at them.

Equity, on the other hand, recognizes that each individual faces different circumstances. Equity acknowledges that not everyone begins in the same place in society. Equity recognizes that some people face adverse conditions and circumstances making it more challenging to achieve their goals. Equity, therefore, allows resources and opportunities to be reallocated in order for these individuals to reach their potential.[lxxviii]

So what does this mean? No two people are the same, no two people face the same conditions, circumstances, or criteria even if given the same things (conditions, possessions, objects, factors, etc.) in the beginning. Equality then is indistinguishable, intangible, and a moving target in a secular world. Yet, some geniuses and gender groups demand equality of opportunities, equality of pay, and equality of benefits for all or at least for their paying supporters regardless of background, education, talent, or other circumstances. They also demand these things regardless of the gender factor, work involved, working conditions, or societal traditions.

In Paul's proclamation of equality to the Galatians he accepted the fact that people have different roles to play in society. He accepted the fact that people are different. However, he also declared that all believers are equal in God's sight no matter who they are, what their occupation, what their gender, or where they came from.[lxxix]

Jesus talked about equality in the book of Matthew where the householder hired laborers throughout the day. Yet, he paid them the same at the days end. He hired them for the same wage regardless of the time worked. For him, it was equal. For the laborers, it was unfair. So it all came down to perception.[lxxx]

Paul in his letter to the Philippians wrote that Jesus never thought of Himself to be equal to God even though He was God come in the flesh. Therefore, we should not be on an ego trip trying to compare equality to others. We should not commit our efforts out of strife or boastfulness, but in humility and modesty appreciating others who are better than ourselves and for what they provide.[lxxxi]

BOLAND

BIBLE STUDY

Philippians 2:6

> Who, being in the form of God, thought it not robbery to be equal with God:

2 Corinthians 8:13-15

> For I mean not that other men be eased, and ye burdened. But by an equality, that now at this time your abundance may be a supply for their want, that their abundance also may be a supply for your want: that there may be equality. As it is written, He that had gathered much had nothing over; and he that had gathered little had no lack.

Please answer the following questions:

- What does the scripture mean by equality?
- How does this apply to how we use the word?

WOMEN

ROLES

No man takes honor unto himself,
but he that is called of God,

Hebrews 5:4

Women have played, continue to play, and will always play important roles in life, in the home, and in the church. Consider the following:

Financial Supporter

In several gospel accounts, Jesus is said to have traveled from several towns and villages proclaiming the good news of the kingdom of God. His entourage included several women namely Mary (called Magdalene), Joanna the wife of Chuza, the manager of Herod's household, Susanna, and many others. These women were among His followers, who supported Jesus out of their own means.[lxxxii]

Help Mate

God's original design was that women were the helpers suitable to come alongside the men.[lxxxiii]

Example: Before Men

Paul stated that as Christ set the example for the church so also wives should set an example before their husbands in everything. In return the husband will love his wife as he loves himself. The husband, if not a believer, would even be converted by her conduct.[lxxxiv]

Example: Before Church

Women should be an example of appropriate quietness, raising her family, instructing younger women about faith, love, and holiness with dignity.[lxxxv]

Example: Before Others

Because the pagan world was looking closely at the fledgling religion with critical eyes and even our own secular world view Christianity with distain. Paul writes to women to watch their conduct. To the older women, he encourages them to behave with reverence, respect, and virtue; not as gossips, false accusers, or intoxicated with wine. He goes on to say that they should teach younger women the things of God. Such as being sober, loving their children, to be discreet and chaste in public. Understand and respect their role in the family and at church; plus respect their husbands God given roles. Study and apply the word of God that God may be not blasphemed.

<u>Hospitality with Priorities</u>

Martha opened her home to Jesus but became overly concerned with the preparations at the cost of her quality time with the Lord. Jesus message is not to be so worried and upset about the arrangements and the planning of life. We should know when to stop and spend time with God, for that will not be taken away from us.[lxxxvi]

Teacher

Paul instructs the older women to be teachers of the younger women, to be reverent in the way they live, not to be slanderers or addicted to much wine, only to teach what is good. He encourages the younger women to love their husbands and children, to be self-controlled and pure, to be busy at home, to be kind, and to be dependent on their husbands, so that no one will malign the word of God.[lxxxvii]

Gatekeeper

God created both men and women. Then women are not independent of men, nor is men independent of women. Everything comes from God. They are both dependent on God for life, breath, and instruction. God gave overall responsibility of the family to the men. God gave the responsibility of child rearing to women.[lxxxviii]

A Stabilizing Force

For God is not a God of disorder but of peace as in all the congregations of the Lord's people. Both men and women should know when it is best to speak and best to be quiet in the church. For decorum sake, it is better to discuss controversial issues at home before starting unconfirmed matters before the church.[lxxxix] If an issues is among individuals that is where it should be settled, not brought before the church which could create division.

Servant of the Church

In the old testament there certainly were prophetess.[xc] In the New Testament was Phoebe, a deaconess of the church in Cenchreae? Who really knows? However, she did have a role in serving the church as did other women Paul pointed to in his writings. It is a fact that women have important and crucial roles of service in the church.[xci]

<u>Wife & Mother</u>

God's Word says that the role of a wife and mother carries with it a noble title. It is an occupation where her husband and family have full confidence in her and lack nothing of value.

The family call her blessed and praise her! Those who know her respect her. Whether working from home or not, she is known for her intelligence in business. She gets up early and stays up late. She is known for work ethics. She is known for hospitality. She is known for compassion for others. She is known for taking care of family and those in need. She is dignified, wise, instructive, and is not idle. She is neither pretentious nor deceitful.[xcii] Scripture makes it clear how God views a wife and mother.

- She is a virtuous woman
- She is a crown to her husband.[xciii]
- She is a blessing.
- She comes from God..[xciv]
- Do not deal deceitfully against her.[xcv]

- Whosoever divorces his wife and remarries commits adultery.[xcvi]
- Love your wife as yourself.[xcvii]
- Be the husband of only one wife.[xcviii]
- Husbands be good, honor, and delight in your wife that your prayers are not hindered[xcix]
- Husbands guarantee your wife food, clothing, and marital rights before God.[c]

Source of New Life

God makes it clear in His Word that the womb of women is blessed, sacred, and has a divine design.[ci]/[cii] David makes it clear that God creates life in the womb.[ciii] He goes on to say that God knows us before we are formed. God knew us then, before we came out of the womb. God blessed us and designed our lives for a purpose before we were born.[civ] Elizabeth, Mary's cousin even blessed Jesus before He is even born.[cv]

<u>Widow</u>

God declares that "pure religion" before God is to visit the fatherless, visit widows in their affliction, and to keep oneself unspotted from the world.[cvi] God most definitely cares for the fatherless children, true widows, and the strangers.[cvii] God makes a point that by doing this we are doing well, seeking justice, relieving the oppressed. God reiterates the point over again that we are to be there for the fatherless and plead for the true widow.[cviii] Jesus even commended the widow who brought all she had to the Lord's storehouse.[cix] God's Word points out that all true widows are important! [cx] So, what is a true widow? Paul established the qualifications for a true widow as follows:

- They do not have young children at home, if they do:
  - They should remarry,[cxi]
  - They should depend on immediate family, not the church or community.[cxii]
- They are threescore years old (60) or older,
- They were the wife of one man[cxiii]

<u>Warrior</u>

1. Deborah was the only female judge of Israel. Deborah became a warrior after she delivered the word of God to Israelite commander Barak that he was to attack Canaanite General Sisera on Mount Tabor. However, she went into battle with him after he declared, *"If you go with me, I'll go; but if you won't go with me, I won't go."*[cxiv]

2. Jael was the wife of Heber the Kenite. Heber moved his family near Jabin King of Hazor. Jabin was General Sisera's boss, and there was peace between Heber and Jabin. As his army was losing to Barak, Sisera fled on foot and came upon the tent of Jael. Jael drove a tent peg all the way through Sisera's temple and into the ground as he slept. Later Barak came by her tent in his pursuit of Sisera. Jael presented the dead Sisera, the tent peg and all to Barak. There is no doubt she acted as a

warrior. She fulfilled the prophecy of Deborah quickly and completely.

3. Hadassah was her Hebrew name but she is known to biblical history as Esther. The Israelites were held captive in Persia (known today as Iran). The entire nation of Israel was at risk of losing their lives, because of an evil plot. Esther risked everything, including her life, to save the Jewish people. She did everything she could to appeal to the king, from her dress to her actions. She even publicly confessed she was Jewish, putting her life on the line. Mordecai told her that God had placed her there "for such a time as this." this is probably the most famous verse from the Book of Esther.[cxv] When the Jewish people celebrate Purim, they remember how heroically Esther fought to save her nation.

Prayer Warrior

After the ascension of Jesus believers continued with in prayer. Many were women like Mary the mother of Jesus, and other female family members.[cxvi]

In his letter to the Romans Paul extended personal greetings to many of the Christians and "co-workers" in Christ who lived or had fled to Rome. Out of the 29 people Paul mentions, or "salutes", many of them are women who he considered his prayer warriors!

Deacon

In his charge to Timothy, Paul makes it a point that a man must be the husband of only one wife, not a polygamist. This point has been argued for centuries that they should not be divorced, but if you understand the circumstances of the era where polygamy was accepted by the pagan religions of their day that point makes sense. It is obvious that a man's qualifications as a deacon is based on the qualifications of his wife and the conditions of his household.[cxvii] Therefore, when Apollos was instructing others based on only the baptism of John it was not only Aquila who took him aside and explained God in Christ more perfectly, it was his wife Priscilla also! [cxviii]

Prophetess

When Paul came unto Caesarea he entered into the house of Philip the evangelist, where he was met by Philip's four daughters who all had the gift of prophecy. [cxix]

Servanthood

Paul commended Phebe, not only a prominent businesswoman but who was also a strong church leader. It is said she took Paul's letter to the Roman church.

She was travelling to Rome on business. She served a prominent role helping others in the church which is at Cenchreae.[cxx]

<u>Prisoner for Christ</u>

Andronicus and his wife Junia were imprisoned along with Paul for sharing Christ. Paul called them his fellow-prisoners, who are of note among the apostles, who also were in Christ before him.[cxxi]

In Foxe's Book of Martyrs women were presented with appropriate behavior patterns. The ideals for women in the Renaissance were basically the passive Christian virtues such as modesty, humility, sweetness and piety. Foxe was certainly concerned with these Christian virtues for women; however, in certain ways his positive examples of strong women not only reinforced, but also modified that point of view.

Laborers in the Lord

Paul saluted Tryphena and Tryphosa. They must have been conspicuous in the service of the church at Rome. Otherwise Paul would not have singled them out and expressed gratitude for their devoted labor in the Lord.

Paul recognized Philologus and his wife Julia, including Nereus and his unnamed sister for their efforts in spreading the Word of God.

Martyrdom

A martyr is someone that suffers persecution and death for advocating, renouncing, or refusing to renounce or advocate, a religious belief or cause as demanded by those in control of the religious thought. After Christ's ascension, Stephen was the first martyr. However, many more men and women followed over the years. Felicitas was killed in A.D. 162 after watching her seven sons die for their faith.   Perpetua   died   in A.D. 203 in modern day Carthage, Tunisia in Northern Africa as part of a celebration for the emperor.   Foxe's book of martyrs tells the account of multiple men and women dying in during the 16th and 17th century in such   horrible ways for simply not complying to the rules of the controlling religious rulings of the day.[cxxii] Then there was a group called the Waldensians who were   adherents   of   movement   within Western   Christianity   before   the   full Reformation got started.   Their teachings came into conflict with the ruling Catholic Church. In a series of persecutions many unnamed men, women and children were martyred because of their beliefs.[cxxiii]

BIBLE STUDY

Proverbs 31:13 (KJV)

> She seeketh wool, and flax, and
> worketh willingly with her hands.

(MSG)

> She shops around for the best
> yarns and cottons and enjoys
> knitting and sewing.

Proverbs 31:15 (KJV)

> She rises also while it is yet night,
> and giveth meat to her household,
> and a portion to her maidens.

(MSG)

> She's up before dawn, preparing
> breakfast for her family and
> organizing her day.

Proverbs 31:17 (KJV)

> She girds her loins with strength and strengthens her arms.

(MSG)

> First thing in the morning, she dresses for work, rolls up her sleeves, eager to get started.

Psalm 23 (KJV)

> Man goes forth unto his work and to his labor until the evening.

(MSG)

> Meanwhile, men and women go out to work, busy at their jobs until evening.

Please answer the following questions:

- Why is there such a differences in the interpretation of the role women between King James and the Message?

WOMEN

CONCLUSION

If your life honors the name of Jesus,
He will honor you.

2 Thessalonians 1:12 (MSG)

So, how should I conclude this study on the life and times of women in scripture? Contrary to the opinion of some, scripture paints a very high opinion of women. It recognized their work. It acknowledges their achievements. It places high value on their contributions to the church of Christ. Even the apostle Paul speaks glowingly of certain women as his fellow-laborers.[cxxiv] He points out many women in his long list in Romans.[cxxv] They are remembered because of their hard work and efforts for Christ. We must not neglect to study what the Old and New Testament women did. We must not forget what God requires of everyone in the church today. All true believers, whether they be men or women:

- Are to be His witnesses,
- Are to share what they learn with others,
- Are to help those who need help when it is in their power to help,
- Are to be faithful in prayer,
- Are to avoid meaningless debates
- Are to love one another.

Even so, the undeniable truth of the Bible is that God has assigned to men the responsibility of leadership. There is, however, strong evidence of spiritual equality and unity between men and women. Where inequality and gender issues come into play the culprit is simply Satan and the sin factor. With the existence of sin, men either choose to rule aggressively or abandon their responsibility. In the former, it is expressed by autocracy, demagoguery, or superiority. In the latter, it is observed by the complete abandonment of their God given responsibility. In either case women have to either defend themselves from aggressive male egos or take up the mantle of responsibility and take charge. In either case this is not how God intended life to function. The example of Christ was one of love and self-sacrificial leadership.

Christ exemplified the idea of leadership which did not mean doing everything alone. Neither did the idea of submission mean being helpless and docile. Consider Jesus example:

- Jesus understood His role as God's sacrificial lamb.
- Jesus was obedient (submissive) to God's Will.
- Jesus action was God being triumphant over the sin factor.[cxxvi]

So should women be a minister or priest? There are two schools of thought. One is the definitive "No" Conclusion! This resonates loud and clear with the conservative school of thought. Men over the past two-thousand years have interpreted the following facts:

- God told man he was responsible for humanity.[cxxvii]
- Jesus only "named" apostles were male. (Fact: women were there!) [cxxviii]
- New Testament passages cite an absolute prohibition of a ministerial role for women[cxxix]
- Then there is the vague argument related to a so-called natural order that women should forever be subservient to men.[cxxx]

- Finally, there is the notion since the scriptures continually refer to and use the male gender it means what it says.

  This statement, however, forgets the fact that in Hebrew and Greek gender is viewed as a grammatical attribute of a noun. It does not necessarily indicate a person, animal, or thing.

Then there is the "Yes" Conclusion! This is the other side of the argument of where women can be ministers and priests. Many liberals and feminist interpret the New Testament prohibitions simply as practical advice to the first century church in order to preserve the sanctity, tranquility of the church community and avoid any form of scandal.

As previously pointed out many great leaders and prophets of Israel were women. It makes one wonder if then God really intended to exclude women from spiritual and political leadership. Shouldn't Paul's statement of equality and Jesus' willingness to defy convention by accepting women into His inner circle be our guiding principle? It is a fact that women had a large role to play in the early leadership of the church. So it seems that women today should be able to serve the Church in whatever positions they are qualified to fill. Key term "qualified"!.[cxxxi]

Final thoughts

Scripture states a wise woman builds her house but the foolish tears it down.[cxxxii] It must be added, a wise husband goes beyond the scriptural meaning for his wife.

- Being there daily for her both professionally and personally.
- Setting an example of love, cooperation, and equality before their children.
- Being content with his wife and not to look at women as lustful objects of pleasure.[cxxxiii]

Scripture goes on to say that a woman who put more effort into seeking God than beauty is worthy of praise and honor.[cxxxiv] Scripture instructs us to prioritize the things of God rather than earthly things.[cxxxv] Scripture says not to compare ourselves to others but be content with how God made us.[cxxxvi]

At the start of each Jewish Shabbat meal the song *"Eishet Chayil,"* is song, which is a tribute to a Jewish woman as written by King Solomon.[cxxxvii] This comes from the Proverb which praises a woman's wisdom and hard work as she makes her home a lovely and nurturing place.[cxxxviii]

BOLAND

BIBLE STUDY

Matthew 5:28

> But I say unto you, that whosoever
> looks on a woman to lust after her
> hath committed adultery with her
> already in his heart.

Proverbs 5:18

> Let thy fountain be blessed and
> rejoice with the wife of thy youth.

Proverbs 14:1

> Every wise woman builds her house:
> but the foolish plucks it down with
> her hands.

Philippians 4:3

> I intreat thee also, true yokefellow,
> help those women which labor with
> me in the gospel, with Clement also,
> and with other my fellow laborers,
> whose names are in the book of life.

Please answer the following question:

- Does scripture place women in high regard or not?
- What does it mean to treat a women with respect and dignity?

WOMEN

BOLAND

BIBLIOGRAPHY

INTRODUCTION

[i]

Genesis 1:27

[ii]

Exodus 21:15, 17, 28–31; Numbers 5:19–20, 29; 6:2; 30:1–16

[iii] https://www.gracechurch.org/about/distinctives/role-of-women

[iv]

Matthew 13:33; 22:1–2; 24:41; Luke 15:8–10

[v]

Matthew 10:34

[vi]

John 4

[vii]

Luke 10:38

[viii]

Ephesians 5:21

[ix]

Ephesians 5:22; Colossians 3:18; Titus 2:5; 1 Peter 3:1

[x]

Genesis 1:27

[xi]

Ephesians 5:25

[xii]

Ephesians 6:4; Colossians 3:21; 1 Timothy 3:4–5

[xiii]

Titus 2:5

[xiv]

Acts 1:12–14; 9:36–42; 16:13–15; 17:1–4, 10–12; 18:1–2, 18, 24–28; Romans 16; 1 Corinthians 16:19; 2 Timothy 1:5; 4:19

[xv]

Romans 16; Philippians 4:3

xvi

1 Timothy 2:12

xvii

25+ Biblical Roles for Biblical Women, (2013), https://margmowczko.com/25-biblical-roles-for-biblical-women/

xviii

Micah 6:4

xix

Exodus 1:15-22, 2:5-10; 2 Samuel 4:4

xx

2 Kings 11:1-3

xxi

Exodus 38:8; 1 Samuel 2:22

xxii

Exodus 4:24-26, 1 Samuel 19:11-17, 25:1

xxiii

Genesis 38:26; Ruth 4:12; Matthew 1:3

xxiv

Joshua 2:1, 6:22-25

xxv

Numbers 26-27, 36; Joshua 17:3; 1 Chronicles 7:15

xxvi

2 Kings 22:14; 2 Chronicles 34:22; Nehemiah 6:14; Isaiah 8:3

xxvii

Judges 4:17-22; 5:24-27, 13:6-10

xxviii

Judges 4:17-24,13:1; 1 Samuel 25:28; 2 Kings 4:8-37; Luke 1:18

xxix

Ruth 3:7

xxx

2 Chronicles 34:19-33; 2 Kings 22:8-20, 23:1-25

xxxi

1 Chronicles 7:24 Nehemiah 3:12

---

xxxii

1 Kings 10:1, Esther, Acts 8:27

xxxiii

1 Kings 17:8-24; Luke 4:35-36

xxxiv

2 Kings 5

xxxv

Genesis 29:9; Exodus 2:16; Joshua 15:17-19; Ruth 2:8; Acts 16:14; 18:3

xxxvi

Exodus 15:19-21, Judges 11:34, Jeremiah 9:17-20

xxxvii

Exodus 15:20-21, Judges 5:1, 1 Samuel 2:1, Luke 1:46, Luke 1:41

xxxviii

Proverbs 31:1, Luke 2:37-38, Acts 18:26

xxxix

John 20:1-18

xl

Acts 16:40, Colossians 4:15,1 Corinthians 16:19, 2 John 1:1, 5

BLESSED

xli

What Does It Really Mean to Be Blessed? By Sarah Walton, (2015) https://unlockingthebible.org/2015/11/what-does-it-really-mean-to-be-blessed/

xlii

The American Heritage College Dictionary, 3rd Edition, Houghton-Mifflin Company, Boston (1993)

xliii

https://www.blueletterbible.org/lexicon/g3107/kjv/tr/0-1/

xliv

Genesis 1:22, 28; 5:2

xlv

Genesis 24:60

xlvi

Genesis 30:13

xlvii

Genesis 31:55

xlviii

Deuteronomy 7

xlix

Deuteronomy 28:3-14

l

Judges 5:24

li

Ruth 3:10

lii

Ruth 4:14

liii

1 Samuel 2:20

liv

1 Samuel 25

lv

Proverbs 31:28

lvi

Song of Solomon 6:9

lvii

Luke 1:28, 42, 45

APPEARANCE

lviii

Deuteronomy 22:5

lix

Romans 12:1-2

lx

Vine's Expository Dictionary of Old & New Testament

Words
By: W.E. Vine Thomas, Thomas Nelson Publishing, (2003)
lxi

Strongest Strong's Exhaustive Concordance of the Bible,
21st Century Edition, By James Strong, Zondervan (2001)
lxii

1 Timothy 2:9-10 (CJB)
lxiii

1 Timothy 2:9-10; 1 Peter 3:3-4
lxiv

Philippians 4:8; 1 Corinthians 6:19-20; Romans 13:14;
Ephesians 4:24; Galatians 3:27
lxv

Workplace Rewards Tall People With Money, Respect, UF
Study by Sarah Raynes, (2003)
https://news.ufl.edu/archive/2003/10/workplace-
rewards-tall-people-with-money-respect-uf-study-
shows.html
lxvi

Overweight? You May Be Getting Paid Less
A report released by George Washington University says
obese women get paid less than normal-weight
coworkers.
Written by Melissa Romero (2011)

Preventing Childhood Obesity
Health in the Balance
Institute of Medicine (US) Committee on Prevention of
Obesity in Children and Youth; Editors: Jeffrey P Koplan,
Catharyn T Liverman, and Vivica I Kraak.
Washington (DC): National Academies Press (US); 2005.
ISBN-10: 0-309-09196-9ISBN-10: 0-309-09315-5
lxvii

https://cms.qut.edu.au/__data/assets/pdf_file/0017/720
53/annual-report-2010-20110915.pdf
lxviii

https://www.scimagojr.com/journalsearch.php?q=20247&tip=sid

lxix

ACE. "Taking Steps to weight loss." Fitness Journal. April 2019: 4-5. Print.
Barlow, S.E., et al. 2007. Expert committee recommendations regarding the prevention, assessment, and treatment of child and adolescent overweight and obesity: Summary report. Pediatrics, 120 (Suppl. 4), S164-92.
Flodmark, C.E. 2016. What's new in childhood obesity and what do we still need to establish? Acta Pediatrica, 105 (10), 116-18.
Kist, C., et al. 2016. Physical activity in clinical pediatric weight management programs: Current practices and recommendations. Clinical Pediatrics, 55 (13), 1219-29.
Ogden, C.L., et al. 2016. Trends in obesity prevalence in the United States, 1988-1994 through 2013-2014. Journal of the American Medical Association, 315 (21), 2292-99.
U.S Preventive Services Task Force. 2017. Screening for obesity in children and adolescents: U.S Preventative Services Task Force recommendation statement. JAMA, 317 (23), 2417-26.
lxx

Study: Cosmetics Significantly Influence Perceptions
By Michelle Denise L. Ferreol, Contributing Writer
October 7, 2011
lxxi

Does Beauty Drive Economic Success? By Adam Alter
The New Yorker, (2013)
lxxii

You Are Judged by Your Appearance by Ty Kiisel
Entrepreneurs, (2013)
https://www.forbes.com/sites/tykiisel/2013/03/20/you-

---

are-judged-by-your-appearance/?sh=20f414c86d50

lxxiii

Romans 12:1-2

lxxiv

1 Thessalonians 2:4

EQUALITY

lxxv

https://www.pewresearch.org/social-trends/2017/10/18/wide-partisan-gaps-in-u-s-over-how-far-the-country-has-come-on-gender-equality/

lxxvi

https://www.cbeinternational.org/resource/article/priscilla-papers-academic-journal/bible-teaches-equal-standing-man-and-woman

lxxvii

The American Heritage College Dictionary, 3rd Edition, Houghton-Mifflin Company, Boston (1993)

lxxviii

"Racial Equality or Racial Equity? The Difference it Makes," Race Matters Institute. (2014) http://viablefuturescenter.org/racemattersinstitute/2014/04/02/racial-equality-or-racial-equity-the-difference-it-makes/

lxxix

Galatians 3:26-29

lxxx

Matthew 20:1-16

lxxxi

Philippians 2:6

ROLES

lxxxii

Luke 8:1-3; Matthew 27:55-56

lxxxiii

Genesis 2:18

lxxxiv

Ephesians 5:22-33; 1 Peter 3:1-6

lxxxv

1 Timothy 2:11-15

lxxxvi

Luke 10:38-42; Acts 18:26

lxxxvii

Titus 2:1-5; 1 Timothy 5:14

lxxxviii

1 Corinthians 11:2-16, Ephesians 5:22-24; Titus 2:4-5

lxxxix

1 Corinthians 1-5, 14:33-35; Ephesians 5:21

xc

Judges 4:4

xci

Romans 16:1, 16:2-27

xcii

Proverbs 31:10-31

xciii

Proverbs 12:4

xciv

Proverbs 19:14

xcv

Malachi 2:15

xcvi

Mark 10:11

xcvii

Ephesians 5:33

xcviii

Titus 1:6

xcix

1 Peter 3:7

c

Exodus 21:10, 1 Corinthians 7:3

---

ci

Genesis 25:23

cii

1 Samuel 1:5

ciii

Psalm 22:9

civ

Jeremiah 1:5

cv

Luke 1:42

cvi

James 1:27

cvii

Jeremiah 49:11; Psalm 146:9

cviii

Isaiah 1:17

cix

Mark 12:42

cx

Acts 6:1

cxi

1 Timothy 5:14

cxii

1 Timothy 5:4

cxiii

1 Timothy 5:9

cxiv

Judges 4:2, 4:8-10

cxv

Esther 4:14

cxvi

Acts 1:12-14

cxvii

1 Timothy 3:12

cxviii

Acts 18:24-26, Romans 16:3-4

cxix

Acts 21:7-9

cxx

Romans 16:1-2

cxxi

Romans 16:7

cxxii

https://www.bl.uk/collection-items/john-foxes-book-of-martyrs
https://www.gutenberg.org/files/22400/22400-h/22400-h.htm

cxxiii

https://museeprotestant.org/en/notice/a-history-of-the-waldensians/

CONCLUSION

cxxiv

Philippians 4:3

cxxv

Romans 16

cxxvi

Conclusions About Women In Ministry, by Rosemary Bardsley 2005, 2015
https://www.godswordforyou.com/women/women-in-the-church/1081-conclusions-about-women-in-ministry.html

cxxvii

Genesis 3:17-24

cxxviii

Matthew 10:2-4, Mark 3:16-19, Luke 6:13-16, Acts 1:13.

cxxix

1 Corinthians 11:3, 14:33-35; Timothy 2:11-12; Ephesians 5:22-23.

---

cxxx

https://www.christianbiblereference.org/faq_women.htm

cxxxi

https://www.christianbiblereference.org/faq_women.htm

cxxxii

Proverbs 14:1

cxxxiii

Matthew 5:28; Proverbs 5:18

cxxxiv

Proverbs 31:30

cxxxv

Luke 7:44, John 6:33

cxxxvi

Romans 1:27

cxxxvii

What to Expect at a Shabbat Dinner, By Nechama Golding
https://www.chabad.org/library/article_cdo/aid/2995074
/jewish/What-to-Expect-at-a-Shabbat-Dinner.htm

cxxxviii

Psalm 31:10-31